Poetic Of

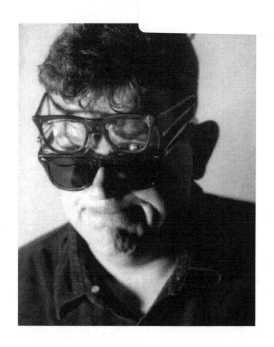

In memory of
Richard Henry McFarlane
(Hovis Presley)
1960-2005

Poetic Off Licence

Hovis Presley

Flapjack Press
flapjackpress.co.uk

exploring the synergy between performance and the page

Published in 2015 by Flapjack Press
Salford, Gtr Manchester
flapjackpress.co.uk

ISBN 978-0-9932370-0-3

First published as *Poetic Off Licence Holiday Annual*
[ISBN 1-9005870-7-5, d2 Digital by Design Ltd, 1997].
Re-issued in the original format as *Poetic Off Licence Bumper Edition*,
with the author's amendments and some additional material
[ISBN 1-9005874-2-4, d2 Digital by Design Ltd, 2005].
Each loosely based on *Poetic Off Licence and Other Likely Stories*
[Billy Scorey Press, 1993].

hovispresley.co.uk

Printed by Lonsdale Direct
Denington Estate, Wellingborough, Northants
lonsdaledirect.co.uk

Dedicated to Nitty Nora the Bug Explorer

Any similarity between characters depicted and real people
and events is a bit odd, bordering on coincidence.
Views expressed are not necessarily anyone else's.
Suitable for vegetarians.
No puns intended.

from the 2005 'Bumper Edition'

Hovis Presley left us all too soon in June 2005. He told some great tales, mixing hilarious lines with brilliant wordplay.

His family and friends have re-published this book as his legacy. Richard (Hovis) loved Bolton and his poetry reflects the idiosyncrasies of everyday life. It is a bonus that the re-sale of this book will generate money for the local charities that Richard held dear and to which he always remained committed.

Spread the word, put it in your pocket and, as Richard would say, "Ta".

Richard's family, 2005

for this 2015 re-issue

This re-issue of *Poetic Off Licence* is based on the 'Bumper Edition' of 2005.

We would like to thank the McFarlane family for their support and for entrusting us with the task of bringing the work of Hovis Presley to a wider audience. Also thanks to Graham Mallinson of d2 Digital by Design who published the earlier versions, Sally for allowing us to use the original cover design, and Bazil for the illustrations (including some new ones).

Proceeds from the sale of this edition will go to support the Hovis Presley Memorial Fund [www.hovispresley.co.uk], which was set up by family and friends to raise money for charitable good works in memory of the author, and Live from Worktown [www.livefromworktown.org], which promotes performance poetry in its many forms.

Dave Morgan, *Live from Worktown*
Paul Neads, *Flapjack Press*

Richard and Dave Morgan at
the Spotlight Club, Lancaster;
'Hovis in Wonderland' CD

contents

brief introduction

evening Jean
evening Fiona
evening Ena
thank you Pauline
hi Jean
hi Fi
hi Ena
ta Pauline

I rely on you

I rely on you
like a Skoda needs suspension
like the aged need a pension
like a trampoline needs tension
like a bungee jump needs apprehension
I rely on you
like a camera needs a shutter
like a golfer needs a putter
like a gambler needs a flutter
like a buttered scone involves some butter
I rely on you
like an acrobat needs ice cool nerve
like a hairpin needs a drastic curve
like a HGV needs endless Derv
like an outside left needs a body swerve
I rely on you
like a handyman needs pliers
like an auctioneer needs buyers
like a laundromat needs driers
like *The Good Life* needed Richard Briers
I rely on you
like a water vole needs water
like a brick outhouse needs mortar
like a lemming to the slaughter
Ryan's just Ryan without his daughter
I rely on you

meet Dave, he swims like a fish

your eyes are like tombola
full of mystery and consolation
your smile is like a parachute
a silk screen of anticipation
your teeth are like teeth
well perhaps a little whiter
your hair is like wild
or some other Irish writer
I could swear that the air
never felt fresher
I don't care what anyone else says
I could listen to your every word
but I'm so busy
vainly trying to impress you
that you never get a chance
to get an edge in wordways
I'd tell you that you're brilliant
but you're too shy to see it
your smile would light the national grid
if you would only free it
you act like no one else on earth
and you're so modest with it
there's one small point
I'd like to mention
when you've got a minute

your boyfriend's a gormless twat
I wish he'd disappear
cos *I did this* and *I did that*
is all I ever seem to hear
all roads lead to romance
but the signpost isn't clear

and your boyfriend's just too normal
to be anything but weird
your boyfriend is just excess flab
one black hole from ear to ear
please return him to the lab
he wasn't such a bright idea
your fuddy duddy bosom buddy
Boris Karloff understudy
cannot comprehend
how could he?
the painful pressing need to dispatch
this plainly pointless kisscatch mismatch
put your sweet lips
a little closer to the phone...

you could only call him pal
cos he looks like a dog's dinner

•

it's a jungle out there

he's like a rhino chasing a jeep
thinks her excuses are tame
she'd rather watch a zebra crossing
wants to put off the wild game
he's got a face that'd
frighten a stonefish
he'd make a crocodile shoo
he said "I make love
like a stampeding wildebeest"
she said "I'll paddle my own gnu"

hey Joe

hey Joe
where you going with that
ratchet screwdriver in your hand?
I'm gonna dismantle my old lady
caught her messin' round
with my Workmate man

your mind's knocked through
to another room
you can't peg it back with a dowel
she can't get through
to this heart of stone cladding
it's time to throw in the trowel

a gentle breeze block blows
the dormer windows of my mind
I find that DIY's
the only way
I can unwind
and if you see home furnishing
as some kind of compulsion
I second that emulsion

ain't too sad
papa's got a brand new gro-bag

mould

don't try to mould me
I don't want to get
set in your ways

a small coupon of my affection

she gave me a smile
from the top of the pile
that made me forget
why I'd called for a while

it's a bolt from the blue
it's too good to be true
that a woman like that
could have eyes just for you

though I have to admit
that if push comes to shove
round here shop assistants
call everyone love

gulp

bacon sausage egg chips
beans mushrooms tomatoes
fried bread and a cup of tea

it's a meal in itself really

**take away that woodstain
and don't darken my door again**

I hate you at sunset
over a Norfolk cornfield
I hate you at sunrise over the Lakes
I hate you when we won at Highbury
I hate you watching Cajun music
on a bank holiday Monday
I hate you at birthdays weddings
Christmas and bar mitzvahs
let's face it...
I hate you at the best of times

ex

i
as good things go
she went

ii
she said
you think the grass is greener
he said
perhaps you should stop watering it

iii
she's grown tired of worlds
to which he is just waking
she's achingly beautiful
he is just aching
they were no longer two peas in a pod
they moved in different directions
she started faking her orgasms
he started faking erections

iv
she once drove him wild
now she just drives him mad
it's the season
for circling personal ads
she sat at home with a nightcap
he tried out different brands
she left but she left him a street map
so at least he knows where he stands

v
Jimmy cracks on that he don't care

are you dancing?

am I just confusing
attention with intention?
affection with attraction?

you lately sent me signals
that are open to interpretation
I'd ask for graphic illustration
but it might cause some aggravation

to every saucepan there's
a lid that fits
don't be too ambiguous
subtle hints cannot
your aims transmit
make it bloody obvious

blanket cover cloud enclosing
camouflaging Winter Hill
silver shining seagull soaring
over distant mill

are you dancing?
no, it's just the way I'm stood

the punter from the blue lagoon

every gimmick's been exploited
freebie t-shirts freak balloons
soap opera celebrities
half price macaroons
now traders in their waders guide you
gently to their craft
as you glide contently round the market
in your personalised shopping raft

cruise the corned beef coral reef
sheltered from the climate nasty
try a free range seafood pizza
or a green algae pasty
at the world's first dive-in restaurant
sales are buoyant fill your boots
everybody's off their trolley
a short shark shop for new recruits
pile 'em high and sell 'em cheap
everything must go
dress John Noakes up as a frogman
Phil Cool as Jacques Cousteau

sorry 'bout the Barndale Centre
everybody makes mistakes
this'll catch the floating voter
keep stilettos off mosaics
wallow in this mayor made heaven
modern leisure's brave new face
shop and swim till half past seven
at the Water Market Place

recipe for adventure

take some lentils up a hill
observe which way the wind is facing
and as you cause the bag to spill
cry "this'll set the pulses racing"

the girl who dances to announcements

the record's long since ended
the DJ babbles on
the girl who dances to announcements
simply carries on
long as there's a song to sing
there's the space to dance
the girl who dances to announcements
takes every cha cha chance
songs that make the senses shudder
songs that make the eardrums strike
gag the DJ hit the deck
confiscate the mic

in this world of mad confusion
uncertainty is rife
the girl who dances to announcements
could dance into my life
compensate each human weakness
nurture any nascent art
praise each humble faltering effort
put the horse before the cart

truth is she's too busy dancing
to take on board a fool like me
spend the evening sideways glancing
thinking of what might have been
TAXI FOR A MR. JOHNSON!
head sways toe tips start to tap
ANYMORE FOR RAFFLE TICKETS?
feel the breeze as shoulders flap
JANICE, RECEPTION PLEASE!

clicking fingers brisk handclap
spinning like a whirling dervish
lands exhausted in your lap
her engine runs on different fuel
the well's run dry it's kind of cruel
and I admit defeat
a man who only plays flamenco
haircut like a guard in Tenko
sweeps her off her feet
dancehalls come and go
but the dance goes on
TODMORDEN!
it's no idle recreation
HEBDEN BRIDGE!
it's a full time occupation
MYTHOLMROYD!
dancing to her destination
HALIFAX!
watch her rise above her station

a fistful of Rennies

struggling contortionist
couldn't make ends meet
decided to call it a day
got the sack from the massage parlour
rubbed people up the wrong way
you don't have to be mad to work here
but I am!
he'd yell at any hint of wages
though hardly workaholic
not touched workahol in ages
capsized he clapped eyes
on a novel franchise
and soon all his energies spent
on a fast food theme restaurant
for the sarcastic
called The Spud-U-Resent
the fudge you begrudge
the pies you despise
the salads you couldn't
give a toss about
it's a triumph
of mind over matter
it's a concept whose time's overripe
let the air ring
with disconsolate chatter
hear the till sing
with each cynical gripe
would you like to order a non-starter?

envious the local baker confectioner
turns troublemaker

tired of all rival's wealth amazing
rushes in with all buns glazing
doughnut forsake me oh my darling…

the cream on the sign
at the scene of the crime
was forensics' vital clue
I'm not so muesli amazed
said PC E272
care for a drink?
no, but I looked after some broccoli once

there goes Frugal Dougal

careful punter market led
bargain hunter born and bred
each night before I go to sleep
I always count discounted sheep
why buy a thing when you can wait
till it has reached its sell by date?
chicken tikka pilau rice
tastes good and cheap at half the price
chicken tikka you and I know…

with no intent to thwart the flab
I basketed all I could grab
can I take it to the fridge?
go ahead take it to the fridge

well I thought I really loved her
then I really wasn't sure
so I grabbed a bag of sausages
and bolted for the door
just telephone me after six
you'll get to know the score
there must be
thrifty ways to leave your lover

thought for Christmas

wait ages for a wise man
then three come at once

a rozzer by any other name

to select a name
for your child
at the first neap tide
after St. Lammas
dance naked
round a white willow tree
bearing a tincture
of mistletoe and ambergris
name the child
after the officer
who arrests you

one for sorrow, Yootha Joyce

the windows were full of compensation
as we headed for Blackpool Eliminations
photographers from the pepperami
watched a man on a Hardly Davidson
taking pre-arranged eggs
to his wife in Nancy Natal Clinic
past students shouting
give Australia back to the Aubergines
life's a bowl of ferrets at our hotel
Bob Hoskins wouldn't drive me away
but you know me
wherever I lay my hat…
that's my hat

glug

discovering that
his beer shampoo
was more Newton & Ridley
than Proctor & Gamble
he thought "right then,
down the hatch"
now he has a hangover
with a clean conscience

Bazil '97

then I saw her face, now I'm an amoeba

oh what a welcome
web she weaves
my common sense
gets up and leaves
I might appear a touch naïve
I've put two arms in the same sleeve
that's how strong my love is

August
and the streets are paved
with pavement artists

your guess is as good as a mile

my bike thinks it's a BMX
it's just a racer what the heck
my friend says he has x-ray specs
there is no substance I suspect
you think that you're a sex object
and then the other sex objects

a legend in his own opinion

Goatface Muldoon
was a man with a plan
when Goatface talks flash
it's no flash in the pan
if one man can flannel
then flannel he can
folks say that Goatface
was that kind of man
he claimed that blue blood ran
each strand of his clan
but no head of state
made a cursory scan
of the state of his head
or the curious span
of a boatrace as smooth
as a broccoli flan
inhabiting another world
beyond our comprehension
in hogwash Goatface found a home
that needs just slight attention

a drastic way to do your shopping
stocking mask demeanour shocking
he robbed his aunty's sub post office
some petty cash some treacle toffee
fine detail gave the game away
he was wearing the jumper
she knitted for his birthday
light-headed
light-hearted
light-fingered

bring back the cat bring back the birch
the cane the rod the pole the perch
thou shalt not smoke or swear or spit
thou shalt not be a little git

shun the Shrewsbury Imbecile
stuff the Dewsbury Fool
you could pole vault at a limbo dance
and not look so uncool
too lazy to shave
too shady for words
he's not the full shilling
or even two thirds
he reckons he's a card shark
but he's desperate at snap
he claimed he was a plumber
but he's never done a tap
you can push a fridge freezer
from Truro to Troon
before you'll get sense
out of Goatface Muldoon

there was a crooked man
and he walked a crooked mile
and he went about his business
with a certain lack of style
stealing candy from a baby
became somewhat of a trial
now he won't have to worry
about the weather for a while

Pearl's B-Force wine bar

the doorman's dickie bow discloses
that he almost might have been
his wan faced withering glance
denounces you as one of the unclean
welcome to a wine bar
where complacency is queen
and the only thing that questions is
the corner quiz machine

my clothes aren't shouting rebel
but they hardly whisper chic
they don't scream outcast extrovert
or cling on with a clique
while I wonder how my trousers
signal how I spend my week
the style obsessed have me assessed
before I even speak

Donald is a health freak
and as miserable as thin
designs all his own stubble
though he hasn't got a chin
his hobbies include paper clips
and reaching red lights faster
he broke his wrist in St. Moritz
and no one signed the plaster

is this shirt a bit ambitious?
do these shoes blush prospects bleak?
in this waterhole malicious
no one dares the truth to seek

I've got less class than chipboard
but I still aspire to teak
and who's to say I've never seen
a menu spelt in Greek?

Tanya's terrific tan
will take some time to tarnish
as it's creosote tomato soup
and seven coats of varnish
her boyfriend calls her Sandy
cos she gets between his toes
the barman calls her Candy
well she's got a toffee nose

the folk whose image costs the earth
at home at work at play
where how you seem means so much more
that what you do or say
a vicious social circle
where the superficial's king
I'm feeling sorry that I spoke
and I haven't said a thing

little boy blue come blow your wages
the cows won't be coming home for ages

the winter of my quite content

the bedroom's cold
the blanket's hot
the wind's getting up
but I'm not
now is the winter of my quite content

French chalk cheese spread

she says sorted
I say flip
I get plastered
watch her sip
she goes raving
while I kip
a smile once skirmished
with her lip
a quiche on her shoulder
instead of a chip
she's Belgian chocolate
I'm Walnut Whip
wine and soda
sherbet dip
is this a trend
or just a blip?
my partner's too hip
for this partnership

Lucy in the sky with hummus

you've got Black Forest lips
vol-au-vent hips
chicken drumsticks for thighs
first time I saw you
thought tortilla chips
you've got bride
on her wedding night eyes

your eyebrows are the pop-up toasters
cheeks the cups with matching coasters
hair the Sergeant Pepper poster
that's taken us all by supplies

best man's Jim Petty
bridesmaid's called Betty
usual dress code applies
Peter Bonetti can't catch the confetti
though his hands are too sweaty he tries
champagne corks pop on the wild Serengeti
you've got bride
on her wedding night eyes

wedding frock is gingham red
disco 'Jackie Wilson Said'
groom is whisked off
to the marital bed
suit pockets full of whist pies
and wishes he'd room
for the haddock in bread
but it's hard to find suits of that size
the first time I saw you
the wedding bells sang

48

you've got bride
on her wedding night eyes

well what about living together?
I shout as you get off the bus

the slob from Planet Crud

the restless reptiles left the mud
evolving up the tree
the zestless slob from Planet Crud
regressed to the settee
with hair of matted brillo pad
and blood group Dungeness B
his spaced out gaze locked firmly onto
Children's ITV
he's a universal problem
and the Vulcan League agree
as he looked up from his three day growth
and mumbled "where's me tea?"

earthwoman brought primordial soup
and placed it on his knee
but gratitude's an alien concept
to slobjects such as he
the bleak eclipse then licked his lips
Crud code from the crater
Green Man Blue Moon Club Eastern Star
materialising later
and with that he boldly went
returned when each last zob was spent
no astral gastric acid
can compete with what's inside
no cosmetic in the cosmos can
his Crud complexion hide
ask the Daleks dial direct
they won't disagree
he still needs Max Factor
at warp factor three

he's an extra-detestable
extra-terrestrial

there's no big red book here
from Eamonn Android
he's the past tense
you'd prefer to avoid
no satellite is set alight
when slobstacle walks in
by Jupiter when he's around
the atmosphere is thin
and somewhere in Aquarius
Uhura turns to Jim
and queries: *Captain*
why's she going out with him?

highly illogical

Manchester

0161 and half a dozen of the other

double edged ode

I was my own
worst enemy

until I met you

the yellow rose of Tesco

for all my life I've scoured the world
for a lover of football
who loves Uncle Joe's mintballs
and is 5' 7" tall
more lively than a buzzard
itching on a windy tree
surprisingly I've met no one
who fits these categories

I'd love a girl with Irish eyes
who once picked grapes in France
a girl who beats you to the floor
when she asks you to dance
who rolls around in giggling fits
when Groucho's on TV
but I don't think such women drink
in the same pubs as me

I'd like to meet a woman who's
adept at crown green bowls
who's never fancied David Soul
or fainted watching Tony Knowles
these pigeonholes have always proved
too small for tenancy
and uninspired I'm getting tired
of my own company

as if by magic the shopkeeper appeared

dear diary... dull day
nothing ever seems to happen anyway
painted go faster stripes on me cagoule
watched pro-celebrity knock-a-door run
made an old flatcap into a catflap
tried to drink a pot noodle
down in one

my mates are off to Blackburn
to try to find a rave
they seem to think I'm lazy
cos my windowbox is paved
I've tried that disco dancing
and don't think that it agrees
so I'm studying my collection
of the sell-by dates on cheese

recently I had a date
and as we got quite intimate
my wandering hands lovingly gripped her
as she studied the anaglypta
I fumbled swiftly up her back
in a subtle love attack
she asked me "baby what's the crack?"
I answered to her torrid gasps
"I'm trying to undo the clasps"
she signed, replied, a muffled note
"they're on the front on a duffle coat..."

everything that doesn't kill me
makes me stronger
fell of my bike by the dog chew factory
now I can hold my breath for longer

**it's great having the Lake District on your doorstep
until you have to donkeystone it**

an elementary rule of thumb
it's his wife's he's under
what common ground has thrown together
let common sense not put asunder
everything she touches turns to drink
or back onto the wagon
Mary was a little lamb
who turned into a dragon
she's Taurus
with breakfast bar rising
he's the strong silent type
with the emphasis on

uninspiring neighbourhood
uninviting wife
a kind of living I suppose
but not much of a life
escapes the house of hollow glamour
to look up schoolmate in the slammer
from hard-nosed cons and sorry cases
calmly chooses changes places
it's a far far better thing
a far far better diet
and in between the rioting
a bit of peace and quiet

he tried to escape on a donkey
that someone had talked the hind legs off

Manchester Olympics

doves take flight
trumpets blast
Lisa Stansfield sings
and Bobby Charlton's haircut
forms the five Olympic rings

Vidal Sassoon gave Bobby Charlton
some advice
but it went right over his head

karaoke east of Java

the girls call him the survey
he's asked every one in town
opinion's not that varied
and they always turn him down
he enters as the lion tamer
exits as the clown
and he's voted Mr. Average
but he doesn't want the crown
he buys a second hand guitar
to try the three chord brag
it's like a classic walnut dashboard
or the antlers on a stag
no evidence of aptitude
would ever spoil the plot
and he's left to wish
he'd picked a different
copybook to blot
this hapless captive audience
could not have looked so glum
if told "your teeth are perfect
but we'd best take out your gums"
she came in through the bathroom window
left without regret
if music be the food of love
I'll wait for the boxed set

rum and black comedy

it's a kind of love hate relationship
loves to see her
hates to leave
everybody falls for barmaids
sometime in their life
in that tunic see a tonic
lover mistress wife
framed soft focus in the optics
love at fifteenth sight

she hints that there's more
than a counter between them
bitter won't tell him the truth
courting self-conscious
'cross chaperone bar towels
he's blind when surrounded by proof

that she sees other men
when she's stuck to the till
that he won't stick around
when she's over the hill
he's inclined to go Dutch
when he's handled his fill
and the truth is he'd rather
be seeing that Gill

but he's mad about Meagan
it's sad but it's true
he dreams that they'll meet
for a quiet drink or two
mad about Meagan
it's easy to see

he's ordered ten pints
and he's only drunk three
she'll leave in a taxi
he'll cry in his beer
her regular answer
is isinglass clear
to each invitation
she counters
no fear!
and watch you spend all me wages in here?

take me drunk I'm home

I wandered lonely as an insurance salesman...

trying to find eight score draws
for three score years and ten...

"fool's gold"
the waiter replied with a sigh as
I ordered a truckload of pie in the sky
the graph of my progress
just fell off the chart
my life and my trousers
are falling apart

my other trousers are a Porsche
I left them in the batcave
I have visions of St. Michael
but I still end up at Kwiksave
hope is hibernating
optimism's flying south
I wouldn't know a gift horse
if it kissed me in the mouth
my lifestyle's now listed
in *Exchange & Mart*
my life and my trousers
are falling apart
and you can always patch your kecks

the four corners of the seven seas

on it's own mountain trout
unlucky for some frigate mackerel
clickety click ox-eyed herring
eyes down for surrealist bingo

**not so much a leading light…
more a faulty rear indicator**

I can't start my life
won't you lend me a hand?
things never seem
to turn out as I planned
I knew that somebody
like you'd understand
just being myself has become overmanned

years and years of going round in circles
going backwards in a cloud of dust
years and years of being
driven to distraction
waiting for the motor of your trust

I can't say I can't live without you
I seemed to be living before
I just thought that you were
the one person who'd care
to show me what I'm living for

the boundary commission

"how's it going?" the stranger said
disturbed my idle meditation
"not bad" said I reluctantly
and asked as to his situation
"oh I mustn't bloody grumble
I can't really complain
no one ever bothers listening
so it's all the bloody same
the weather's always miserable
it's always sodding rain
you could catch senile dementia
whilst waiting for a train...
beer today's as weak as water
but I'm not one to grouse
I'm only going down the pub
to get out of the house
our back field's a new estate
they call it Pine Tree Heights
the only thing that's ever green
are the bloody traffic lights
that car boot sale over there
that used to be a foundry"
and so I missed the vital catch
whilst fielding on the boundary

my little crony

cigarettes whisky
petrol chocolate
ladies nylons
dirty postcards

I've got a memory like a spiv

roll over Bert Weedon

bigger than The Beatles
there's really no comparison
Dave's taller than McCartney
I'm wider than George Harrison

nuff respect... for now

a face
as sweet as grapefruit
the figure of Geoff Capes
but you'll never catch me
calling you
Janet of the Apes
though I curse
the day you left me
there's no hint
of sour grapes
you'll never catch me
calling for you
Janet of the Apes

mine

it always rains at miners' rallies
our winter weather chills the soul
these islands have a cruel climate
I'm glad somebody's digging coal

the ballad of Baxter's barge

as snowflakes wished the locks goodnight
and flirted with the ground
the Phoenix took another flight
the keeper to astound:
as sure as my authority
is my seafaring beard
to move a barge at 5 a.m.
is radical and weird
but the captain conspires
with his compulsive's plea
let's sail for as far
as the eye cannot see

'twere January '91
and wanton wind did blow
as we set off for the Phoenix
with a yo ho bloody ho
berthed high in the county
where Fred Sewards Trueman's king
it's needed back on Red Rose turf
before the locks all shut till spring
an ungodly hour on the Sabbath day
the atmosphere is tense
can the suspension stand it?
can we stand the suspense?

Baxter's cockahoopie scoop
ridiculously sublime
across the Pennines round the clock
in a three mile an hour race against time
thirteen locks and three swing bridges
derelict mills discarded fridges

Marton Nelson Clayton Rishton
bleakest water ever fished on
the sleet brings an unlikely
tan to our faces
the wind parts your hairstyle
in several places

this blistering blizzard
that chatters and chases
chastens your taste
for the wide open spaces
Jack Kerouac pack your plastic mac
and join our merry crew
you'll be taken aback by the total lack
of owt better to do
and with the passing of each year
as folk do reminisce
each arcane angling anecdote
each fleeting flickering furtive kiss
they'll gaze abstractly into space
with numbness only I could miss
and wonder *will we ever hear
the bloody end of this?*

Tranquility Base
the seagull has landed

I'll burn that bridge when I come to it

I was chattering merrily
yet pertinently
when suddenly
without repentance
she did what most jailbirds
wish they could do
and walked off in mid-sentence

well I'm the kind of guy
who'll never shut his trap
where pretty girls are
you'll find me talking crap
they call me the mitherer
the meanderer
I witter on and on and on and on

repeat repeatedly

it's phonely love…

<SORRY, ROBERT ISN'T IN AT THE MOMENT>

you know that I've no wish
to answer your call
you don't rush to catch me
whenever I fall
our carefree freewheeling's
become a long haul
your stream of smooth talk
a meandering drawl

<BUT LEAVE YOUR NAME AND NUMBER>

your finer feelings
are hard to recall
there's more fish in the sea
you so tactlessly trawl
your wandering eye is
a foul off the ball
so go pick another
prize off the stall

<AND HE'LL GET BACK TO YOU SHORTLY>

I'd come running back
but you want me to crawl
it feels more appealing
to rot on Rockall
this battle of wits
is a blundering brawl
this could be the start
of something small

<PLEASE LEAVE YOUR MESSAGE NOW>

mmmmmmmmmm

oh drop dead

Cornish postcard

sun sea
sand sex
well three out of four ain't bad

come back and start what you finished

I really thought that my ship had come in
thought you were Helen of Troy
but now distraught
is the shape that I'm in
as you shop for a new toy

I'm overwrought and my only defence is
I've taken compassionate
leave of my senses
acting intense
there's no need to rehearse
my state of mind's fifth gear in reverse
it's a crying shame

if there's a homeopathic
cure for heartache
I think I need a double dose
I found a recipe for heartbreak
tastes like raw liver on burnt toast
don't want to battle with the bottle
don't want to sulk for seven years
don't want the vacuum filled with valium
don't want no trace
of the tracks of my tears

perfect match

his latest flame's a football fan
the flair of Cruyff the elder's Dutch
a vision of Pele's Brazil
a beautiful first touch

no selection worries now
as seasons far ahead they see
a flask of scotch
a book on Hurst and thou
a pie and a beef tea

go quietly...

beneath this fact of chiselled granite
wreckless Derek Deacon lies
his bold approach to tasks electric
transmits a beacon to the skies
high on drama and theatrics
hooked on greasepaint catering size
bequeaths his loving widow Janet
his Pontins fancy dress first prize

an undiscovered famous actor
luck conspires the fates contrive
forgot the script to fill with colour
this mortal coil in which we strive
career progression like a pinball
useless in the nine-to-five
without him life will be much duller
thank God he never learnt to drive

wild orchids wouldn't drag me away

I seem to be swimming
through oceans of nonsense
to find the truth of your shore
I seem to be running through
a field of confusion to find
the warmth of your door
I seem to be floating off
up to the ceiling
can't keep my feet on the floor
I rest my case
but you're fiercely appealing
you're a hard woman not to adore

I seem to be waiting
at infinite bus stops
waiting for you to pass by
how do I get into this situation?
am I too late to apply?
it's clear there's a window
of caution between us
sometimes I can't see through the pane
I'm stuck in a siding
just give me a signal
and I'll be the guard on your train

everyone deserves a second chance
give me one more try
if you're going to change the world
why not start with mine?
everybody needs someone to love
the average bat can see
everybody needs someone to love
so why not pick on me?

Cathy you know it's time you ought
to get aboard this train of thought
fly from the oche Cupid's dart
and warm the crabsticks of my heart

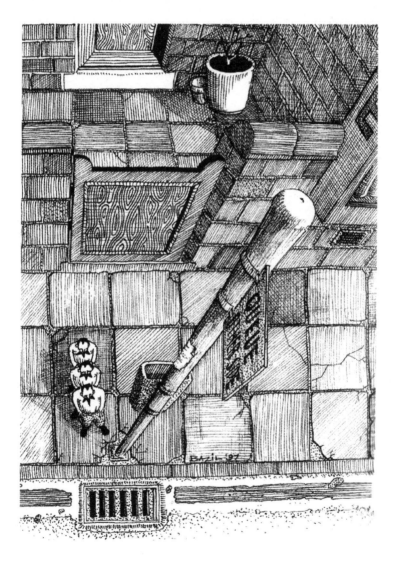

are you lonesome tonight?

four crisp white lights
like highly trained fireflies
glide patiently across the cloudless
chill October night
is that an aircraft or a spaceship?
there's not much call for crop circles
in this stiff neck of town

young folk look on
a little apprehensive
rocket fuel is expensive
if they've come light years
to this chaotic oasis
what's the reason why?
do they seek to fraternise?
initiate some fruitful dialogue
or grab whatever's out of stock
in their cosmic Argos catalogue?

two old men outside their flats stand watching
the bold fluorescent southern drift
a Dansette that's seen better days
plays 'You Were Always On My Mind'
standing lonely on the balcony
hungry for some company
they dream he's landing
on this landing
Elvis, if you're on that spaceship
come on down...

doctor doctor

doctor I have trouble
pronouncing effs and tee aitches

well you can't say fairer than that

over my bed Doddy

whilst steering a wagon
along the M5
I suddenly realise
I've not learnt to drive

I win a verruca
in a lucky dip
I'm chasing the kitchen
it gives me the slip

mindful of this minefield
of subconscious ballyhoo
I'd be reasonably ungrateful
to see all my dreams come true

sun-dried tomatoes and mushy peas

He stomped impatiently round the bedroom
and bellowed tersely, "Where's me effin' pants?
Where's me jeffin' socks? Where's me effin' and
jeffin' shirt?" He'd always been a snappy dresser.

Philosophy student Anita Mullitova took it all
in her stride, like a rag rug to a bull. Though they'd
tripped the light sarcastic more often than she'd
wished, she knew his heart was in the right place.

For her birthday she'd asked him for something
romantic yet practical, and sure enough he'd
produced a negligé with a pocket for garden shears.

He met Anita at the Ideal Comb Exhibition
one mainly rainy day. Photography wasn't permitted,
so he was stubbornly doing some brass rubbings
when she asked him where there was a toilet.
"There's one in my caravan in the Lake District,"
he gratuitously namedropped.

"What's the difference between a twelve course
Chinese banquet and an egg butty?" he said.
"I don't know," she replied. "Do you want to
come round for your tea?" he asked.

And she voted with her lips, because she was
head over heels with Grange Over Sands, and
the queue couldn't be any longer up there.
They moved the caravan, 'Whartson Hall' to
Berwick Across The Mersey. Small enough
to think you'd find your mates in town, big enough
not to find them. That was about the size of it.

It was what economists, sociologists and kebab
carousel maintenance men would call 'a bit of a dump'.
Significant social change meant being able to drink
between 3 and 7 in the afternoon. New alehouses were
launched so frequently people shouted at the builders:
"Can you make this your last pub please, lads?"
Drink was the only choice they were spoilt for.

It had been a dreadful football season.
The centre forward had been routinely sent off,
due to his Sonny Liston disposition. "I can't believe
you're not bitter," the chairman told the fans.

The day relegation was confirmed the tannoy played
'Simply The Best'. The only score that would prevent it
being played was 9 on the Richter Scale.

By creative use of colour, the West Stand seats
depicted the club president's face. If enough
of you turned up in black when the gates opened,
you could give him a moustache, glasses or a pipe.

She wouldn't leave for all the mayonnaise in Leigh-on-Sea.
She became an estate agent's rental deceptionist,
and grew to resent the owner, Mrs. Ovafamilia,
who had won prizes for stating the obvious,
and had no better judgement to which to appeal.

Anita had everything: 'come to bed' eyes,
'what time to you call this?' cheekbones and
'you treat this place like a flippin' hotel!' shoulders.
He'd soon get set in her ways.

kipper butties in bed

Herbert Fountain had a PhD in Knocking About, and
was now knocking about with Frugal Dougal, who had
recently left the Army Self-Catering Corps. He had a
slight stoop from constantly pouring homebrew into
pint pots, and believed strongly that letting the bathwater
go cold before letting it out would help heat the flat.

As half of a small but recently formed skiffle duo,
The Miserly Brothers, his rendition of 'Stranger On The Shore'
on comb and paper had brought a tear to many an eye.

A furtive photo of Dougal once disclosed an awkward
navigator's cleavage. Unless you recognised the spot
pattern, you'd never know it was him. But he kept
the picture, because it had marvellous depth of field,
and you never knew when you might want to reply to
a Lonely Hearts advert, and enclose a recent photograph.

They met as kids: Herbert was carrying some toy soldiers
and Dougal offered to hold the fort. He was the only kid
in the street with an Action Man Singer Songwriter, and
had an extensive stamp collection, though some people
said he was all mouth and tweezers.

Herbert was the creative type. He'd designed the pump
action pump and the heated roofrack, and once made a
suit out of aluminium foil, whilst in a reflective mood.

He'd developed the Chip And Pie Diet, and once
married an inventor, but she left him to his own devices.
He looked like a rep for a hangover company, and took
being serious very seriously. Never one to hide his light

under a bus shelter his business card read
Sir Herbert Fountain: man and settee in perfect harmony.

On a trip to Athens, Herbert was told: "Remember,
you're an ambassador for your country." And that's
what he said when they found him in the Consulate.
He returned resolving to beware Greeks bearing grudges.
Dougal loved tourists, especially the French. Well,
they wouldn't want their breakfast, would they?

Never a dim moment, Herbert reflected, as they
launched their bicycle rickshaw courier service.
The vehicle had been lavishly welded by his cousin,
Albert Hindsight, and resembled a shed on a go-kart.

The slogans *The Spoke You Like* and *No More Red Errands*
had been lovingly detailed by the signwriter,
Seymour Wright, but he'd got the wrong end
of the wedge with the company name. 'Weedy Liver'
was close enough, but Herbert resolved never to order
anything by telephone again. "From now on," said Dougal,
"there's not much turning back."

The West Pennine climate had a rhythm of its own.
Rain in the morning, sun in the afternoon,
fog in the evening, and all for under a fiver.
You couldn't wish for finer drizzle.

freshly clutched straws

Same old story. I've always wanted to live in a pad,
but I've ended up living in a gaff. It needs tidying,
but I can't tell junk from clutter. The last time I had
a clear out local bric-a-brac prices plummeted.

Despite my bonsai bank balance, more than often I go for
a Tizer slammer or a low interest lager with my manager,
Tom Pitta, who I met at a workshy workshop in Worksop.

Former leadswinger with the Muckle Mfr. Co.,
he now works for solicitors Boyle Coyle Doyle Foyle,
Hoyle and Royle. As much fun as a millipede
with verrucas, he once tried to patent the long face,
in an attempt to sue anyone else who used it.

Oddly enough, the nearest pubs are all named after
types of dental treatment. There's the Bridge,
the Crown, and the one with the plaque outside.

The owners of the Bridge actively discourage the overweight,
and now employ a chubby checker on the door, so I breathe in
for a few minutes. It takes ages getting served –
the beer is brewed on the premises, to order.

Tonight there's an engagement party in full swing –
Carmen Sharman's marrying the barman, so we do
the Hokey Cokey round a croaky karaoke. Otherwise,
the jukebox is quite curious – 'Decent Old Town',
'Nights In Prestatyn', 'Don't Look Back In Bangor',
'Search For The Biro Beside The Shelf', 'You're So Vague',
'Try A Little Trendiness', 'You Saw The Whole Macaroon'.

Standing by the pistachio dispenser every other Saturday
is temperamental sentimental Natalie Slatterly-Slattery,
queen of the comely anatomy category, latterly reacting
cattily to flattery. I try to impress her with inane football trivia...

You could cut the atmosphere with specialist atmosphere
cutting equipment. She's on her high horse, on the high
moral ground, floating in virtually fat free reality.
I'm as awkward as a comedian dying on stage, with
all the audience wearing their trousers at half-mast.

Well, we all make mistakes. Like the DJ at my cousin's
wedding who played 'You've Lost That Loving Feeling'
for the happy couple to smooch to. I'm on my last legs,
and I didn't even like the first ones. I should go home
and watch a documentary about sleep, but instead stay
and drink like a fish that thinks that Prohibition's about
to be introduced.

Ah, the Rock and Roll lifestyle. I'll never forget the time
I ran out of milk and had to use Marvel. It's about here
I begin to lose the thread, but never mind,
my mate's got a warehouse full of cotton.
Apparently it's all part of life's rich tapestry.

that's enough adventures Ed

two months in a Turkish gaol
waiting for trial
that's where he met Billy Hayes
star of *Midnight Express*
no films about Eddie
just a few lines
in the local press
illegally importing
a motor vehicle
£17 split four ways
selling a Morris Minor
in Asia Minor

bought a fake passport
and attended his own
fundraising function
in a manner akin
to Huckleberry Finn

in a one donkey town in Egypt
a fellah in full peasant kit
asked Eddie where he was from…

"do you know Maxwell's Plum?"
replied the Egyptian
who had studied
at the local Institute
and had questionable
taste in nightclubs
though hardly spoilt for choice.

I've bitten off more than you've had hot dinners

I once spent an evening with Lola or Layla
she said make me breathless
I hid her inhaler

and if it's any consolation...

every cloud has a silver lining
tomorrow's another day
cheer up it might never happen
as they told them in Pompeii
good times just around the corner
it'll all come out in the wash
when you pull your jeans
from the drying machine
you'll realise where you left your dosh
worse things happen at sea it's true
who'd hesitate to refuse
a cabaret by Chris de Burgh
on their Caribbean cruise
maritime calamity must mean pay
two thousand smackers
to hear old chubby cheeseburger
from Kingston to Caracas
a friend once nearly died of thirst
adrift upon the seven seas
the bar was shut they were miles from Holland
as dehydration took its toll
they sank their duty frees
nobody's perfect that's for sure
my dismal past I'd blush to censor
for if man learns by his mistakes
then why aren't I in Mensa?

let's make a record

I don't get out of bed
for less than a cup of coffee
and a fag
so when Ste said "let's make a record"
I thought "fan-flipping-tastic"

when the record's a smash hit
women talk to you for longer
before mentioning their boyfriends

you start to attract groupies
most of whom want to be your aunty
or your niece
but never mind they'll have friends

before you know it you're living in Cheshire
and using shampoo
it's a far cry from singing Laurie Anderson's
'Oh Superman'
at the karaoke

when you're really famous
you get to call your kids interesting names
like Smedley or Flipper

but already too old to die young
you haven't the energy for all this touring
your wife begins to get jealous
suspecting that she's not the only woman
you grumble and complain to

as your ego declares independence
friends are increasingly distant
leaving you with no one to talk to
on the way down

you learn from teletext that your wife has
renamed your children Susan
and David

finally as you lose all your grip on reality

you grow a beard
and think it looks great

scrap the record Ste

lonely heart

intelligent handsome generous man
wishes to meet woman prepared
to believe any of the above

would you credit it?

choreography PHREDD	animation KEVIN GILDEA
key grip RORY MOTION	rostrum camera JONATHAN KEENAN
special effects SHIATSU TRUDY	catering PLUMP
focus puller STAN VERNON	gaffer DEEP PHIL
locations BRENDAN THE MAGIC BRICKIE	continuity MICHAEL CONROY HARRIS
haulage FLAMENCO DAVE	stunt coordinator JEANETTE
properties GLEN THE BODGER	windowbox WHOLE EARTH LANDSCAPES
cinematography SUE TERRY	hair SHARPLES
make up NOT APPLICABLE	wardrobe LAMINATED CHIPBOARD

filmed in tunnelvision

forthcoming attractions include:

The Girl from Little Lever

Morris Chino's a Cherry

Jason and the Lager Louts

I Had Her in Fifth Once
(A Young Man's Tribute to his Pushbike)

The Freudian Slippers

A Mission of Murphy

Cover designer Sally is a signwriter and mural painter.
She once wrote a brief history of the fishtail parka
on the back of a stamp with a magic marker.

Illustrator Bazil's celebrated cartoon strips 'Seth' and 'Twassock'
have been published in *Wisden Cricket Monthly*.
The circus ran away to join him.

The end is listless.